D0177773

GIANFRANCO ZOLA

HEROES

First published in 1997 by
Invincible Press
an imprint of HarperCollins*Publishers*
London

© The Foundry Creative Media Company Ltd 1997 (text)

All rights reserved. No part of this publication may be reproduced,
stored in a retrieval system, or transmitted, in any form or by any
means, electronic, mechanical, photocopying, recording or
otherwise, without the prior written permission of the publishers.

All attempts have been made to contact copyright owners of material
used in this book; in the event of an oversight, the publishers will be
glad to rectify any omissions in future editions of this book.

A CIP catalogue record for this book is available from the British Library.

ISBN 0 00 218818 X

All rights reserved.

Created and produced by Flame Tree Publishing, a part of
The Foundry Creative Media Company Ltd,
The Long House, Antrobus Road,
Chiswick, London W4 5HY.

GIANFRANCO ZOLA

HEROES

Introduction by Robert Jeffery
Main text by David Harding

ON BALANCE, IT SHOULD HAVE been a tight game. Wimbledon, conquerors of Manchester United and riding high in the league, were desperate to make it to Wembley. Chelsea, under the guidance of boss Ruud Gullit, were by no means certain of winning.

One man was to make the difference: Gianfranco Zola. For 89 minutes he tormented the Dons' defence, twisting and wriggling past challengers, deftly playing team-mates into match-winning positions. His skill helped Chelsea go two-up; then, in the final minute, he picked up the ball on the left, cut inside, sold Chris Parry an unbelievably expert dummy before curling it delicately into the low corner. It was a performance that was to go a long way towards earning him the Footballer of the Year award. It took Chelsea to Wembley for the first time since the 1970s.

Gianfranco Zola does not look, on the face of it, much like the genius he has been unofficially crowned by his new-found supporters. At 5' 5" he is noticeably shorter than the vast majority of those he plays against. His hair, long and ungainly, would not grace the catwalks. Yet he remains the most successful Italian export ever.

Zola was born on the island of Sardinia, three weeks before England won the World Cup Final. As a youth he would draw crowds with his mesmerising skill; by his 16th birthday he was signed to small-town club Nuorese as a full-time professional. Progress to the upper echelons of Serie A was slow, but after impressing at Third Division Torres he was snapped up by Napoli to bolster their challenge for the title in 1989.

He found his push for a regular first team place impeded, however, by one Diego Maradona. The Argentinian – widely regarded as the greatest player in the world – was no longer at the peak of his powers, but a formidable tutor for the young Zola. By 1991 Maradona had gone and, given their similar stature and playing style, it was inevitable that Zola would be landed with the tag of the 'New Maradona'. It was a title he only fleetingly lived up to; Napoli were in decline, and despite impressing enough to earn the first of 33 Italian caps, Zola could not fully replace the great man. He left in the summer of 1993 for Parma, where he tasted glory but failed to land a major trophy. A relatively small side, Parma could not hold him for long and in his fourth season he made the move to London as part of Ruud Gullit's Chelsea resurgence.

The transfer fee of £4.5 million now seems a bargain. In his first eight months at Stamford Bridge, Zola dismissed all doubts about his quality with a series of awe-inspiring performances. Against Manchester United, he ran the defence ragged before

beating Peter Schmeichel with a goal of the finest quality. In the international with England, he ran from the halfway line to severely dent the home nation's World Cup hopes. His 18 goals were all from the top drawer of finishing, while his interplay with Hughes, Di Matteo and Vialli was breathtaking. In May, he landed the FA Cup with another superb performance. Zola's is a talent at its very peak.

Robert Jeffery

ZOLA IN ITALY

GIANFRANCO ZOLA IS NOW ONE of the most famous footballers in the world, known the planet over for his shooting, dribbling and passing skills. He has become almost as famous as his mentor Diego Maradona in the art of scoring direct from long-range free kicks. It is almost certain that football fans all over Europe and the world would have seen a Zola special on TV, even if they didn't realise they were watching the pocket-sized genius.

But despite the fact that he is now one of the most recognisable players in the world, Gianfranco Zola made a slow start to his professional career. He didn't play in Italy's top division, Serie A, until aged 23. Just eight years later he has played in a World Cup, European Championships, two European club finals, an FA Cup final, and at the very top in both Italy and England. He may have been a late-starter but Zola knows how to make up for lost time.

The game in Serie A is so tactical that hardly anyone makes an error, which means it is not interesting for the fans and difficult for the players.
Gianfranco Zola

This man has played in World Cups, he's scored here for Italy against England. He's enjoying himself more today than he's ever enjoyed himself.
Des Lynam, on Zola's reaction to winning the FA Cup

GIANFRANCO ZOLA was born on 5 July, 1966. Despite his amazing skills he wasn't born in one of the traditional hot-beds of Italian football such as Milan, Turin or Rome, but in the small village of Oliena on the island of Sardinia – situated to the west of the Italian mainland – where his father ran a bar. The island is where England played their opening group matches in the World Cup in 1990 against Egypt, Holland and the Republic of Ireland.

The main football team on the island is Cagliari, who have spent many seasons in Italy's Serie A. But despite their long-established record in Italian League football, incredibly they let the amazing talent of Gianfranco Zola slip through their fingers. Zola though has made it known that he wants to finish his career in Italy and, more specifically, in the blue and red colours of Cagliari. He may not have started there but he has every chance of hanging up his boots in Sardinia.

I believe I made the right choice. In Italy it is a difficult time for fantasists while in England that kind of player is loved and looked for.
Gianfranco Zola

He makes me look ordinary.
Gianluca Vialli, on Gianfranco Zola

INSTEAD OF making his name with the island's top team, Zola's career had undistinguished beginnings at the small Sardinian club of Nuorese. They were situated in C2, the equivalent of the lower reaches of the Italian Third Division, when Zola began his career with them. In his first season with the club Nuorese were relegated. Zola showed some of his promise, scoring a total of 10 goals in 31 games. If nobody was going to notice Nuorese they were sure going to notice Gianfranco Zola.

With his control, touch and use of both feet he will say 'see you later' and go past you.
Dennis Wise

IN 1986, aged 20, he joined another Sardinian club, Torres, where he enjoyed more success. He scored a total of 21 goals in 80 games for the club and was instrumental in helping the team win promotion to C1 the next season. The club's director, Nello Barbanera, then persuaded the general manager of southern Italy's biggest club, Luciano Moggi of Napoli, to look at Zola. Although Moggi wasn't massively impressed, he liked enough of what he had seen. As a result Napoli concluded one of their best-ever business transactions: paying £200,000 for a footballer who just a few years later would be valued at £8m. Zola was described by one Italian journalist as 'un oggetto misterioso', an unknown quantity, when Napoli signed him.

The two cities, Naples and Parma, are ideal for footballers and important because they provide continuous stimulation. They also have in common their grand passion football and the fact they have great teams.
Gianfranco Zola

AT NAPOLI, Zola established himself as a favourite, and helped the club lift only its second championship title in history at the expense of their hated northern rivals. In a total of 105 games for Napoli, Zola chipped in 32 goals and became a firm crowd favourite.

From Napoli he headed north, playing 102 games for Parma. There he established himself on the national scene and was soon recognised as one of the country's most exciting talents. With Parma he extended his medal collection, winning the European Cup Winners' Cup at Wembley against Antwerp in 1993. In 1995 he was part of the successful Parma side which won the UEFA Cup beating Juventus 2-1 on aggregate. During the same period the club also challenged consistently for the Serie A title. His strike increased to one every two games, scoring 51 goals for Parma. And to prove his value from free kicks, his success rate at scoring from dead ball situations was at a higher ratio than Juventus's French genius Michel Platini. By the time he left Italy for Chelsea, there was no doubt that Zola was one of the country's foremost talents.

Italian players have a very closed life. Football is all their life is. The game is so serious there is no fun.

Gianfranco Zola

ZOLA'S EXPERTISE made him so popular in Italy that he once appeared on TV to plead for the release of a man who had been kidnapped back in his home of Sardinia. And it proved successful! The captors released their hostage after watching Zola on TV. He was also said to have successfully appealed for the return of his family's husky dog which had gone missing when he was playing in Napoli. The dog had been lost and there had been no sightings, but incredibly, after his appeal, the dog was returned in just a few hours!

I play the piano for a bit of fun. I'm not bad but I'm no Elton John and I don't think there's much chance of anyone ever paying to see me in concert! Or Elton playing football for Watford either! I like music but I prefer something gentle to the loud fierce stuff.
Gianfranco Zola

I really enjoy playing football in England but I must admit I miss real Italian pizza so I've created my own.
Gianfranco Zola

Other things are important to me and that is why I like the English way. My son Andrea and daughter Martina have the chance to learn new things.
Gianfranco Zola

ZOLA AND MARADONA

GIANFRANCO ZOLA COULD HARDLY help becoming one of the continent's top players. Throughout his football career Zola has played with some of the most skilful stars in modern European and world football. At Parma he partnered Newcastle's Colombian international Faustino Asprilla, for Italy his fellow strikers have included Roberto Baggio, Casiraghi and Signori from Lazio. And in England he's played alongside Gullit, Vialli and Hughes.

One player, however, stands out above them all – the flawed genius of Argentina's Diego Maradona: one of the greatest players in the history of football. Maradona, the player who could control a football like no other, who practically won the World Cup single-handed for Argentina in Mexico in 1986, who scored probably the best and most controversial goals in World Cup history against England in the quarter-finals. For several years at the end of the 1980s and beginning of the 1990s he was the hero to all Neapolitans as the man who won the club their first ever Serie A League championship. Towards the end of Maradona's turbulent reign at Napoli, the club drafted in another small genius to replace him – Gianfranco Zola.

Maradona used to stay behind after training to teach me how to curl free-kicks. It paid off when I made my debut against Ascoli. I played badly but scored with a free-kick near the end – to find 60,000 fans going mad.
Gianfranco Zola

DESPITE A BAD reputation with opposing fans, Maradona has commanded very little but respect from his fellow players. Zola is no different and claims Maradona as one of the greatest influences of his career. As teachers in the art of beautiful football there are few better than Diego Maradona. Zola was even dubbed 'the new Maradona' and 'little Diego' in his time at Napoli. High praise indeed and especially for Zola who claims the Argentinian is the best player he has ever seen. Despite the fact that Zola had come from a small-time provincial club and Maradona had played for the top sides in Argentina and Barcelona and played in two World Cup championships, the two diminutive diamonds soon struck up a friendship which Zola recalls fondly to this day.

*Diego Maradona is the best player I have ever seen. He had
everything a player could want and was a very good friend
to me in our time together at Napoli. I just remember him
simply as the best player in the world.*
Gianfranco Zola

THE PAIR WOULD practice their free-kicks after proper training, with Zola picking up top tips from the master. It stood Zola in good stead, when on his debut for Napoli against Ascoli, Zola scored the only goal of the game direct from a free-kick in front of 60,000 screaming fans.

The friendship was mutual, with Maradona rating Zola so highly that when he made his final appearance for Napoli on 17 February, 1991, Maradona symbolically handed the Sardinian his coveted No. 10 shirt.

Diego Maradona said that Gullit and Zola are two of the best players in the world and the fact they are both at Chelsea attracted me to sign.
Chelsea's Uruguayan midfielder Gustavo Poyet

ZOLA SPENT a total of two years as understudy to the world's greatest player, not a bad compliment, but also a hard act to follow. But Zola was to become a firm favourite with the incredibly demanding Napoli fans, and helped them win their second Serie A title in 1990. Gianfranco scored two goals in 18 appearances in the championship winning side.

Despite their rapport on the football field, the two men are very different off the pitch. Zola is teetotal, while Maradona has admitted a cocaine problem which begun in the 1980s at Barcelona and was kicked out of the World Cup in the USA in 1994 because he failed a drug test. Maradona finally left Naples in 1991 with many rumours that he had been befriended by the city's mafia, the Camorro.

To show how much Zola had improved as a player with Napoli, the man who was signed for just £200,000 was sold to Parma for £1.4m in 1993. At Parma, he became a household name not only in his native Italy but across Europe, including Britain, where live Italian League games were broadcast. Supporters across the continent were treated to almost weekly displays of Zola's abilities at dead-ball situations and cheeky skills. Parma, under manager Nevio Scala, was a team transformed. Traditionally a small club who had won no major honours, with financial backing they attracted players of the calibre of Zola and Faustino Asprilla to form a fearsome front line. Parma challenged, for the first time in the club's history, for the Serie A scudetto – taking on the likes of AC Milan and Juventus at their fearsome best.

The last player to keep him out of a team was Maradona.
Chelsea captain Dennis Wise

*We only ever saw him at training and he
lived in a fortress the rest of the time. He had
terrible times but was always fantastic to me.*
Gianfranco Zola

FOR MOST, the television was the closest any British fans
had come to seeing Zola. But in 1993 those fortunate enough
to have a ticket for the European Cup Winners Cup Final at
Wembley would have got a tantalising glimpse of his genius:
he came away from the old stadium with another medal. It
was a stadium which was to prove very lucky for Gianfranco
Zola over the next few years – 1993 certainly wasn't the last
time he was to prove a winner at Wembley.

If Maradona went for a walk, the whole city of Naples wanted to touch him, and a lot of bad people began to hang round him.
Gianfranco Zola

It was a flash of lightning. I don't think anyone like Diego will ever be born again. I've learnt so much from just watching him.
Gianfranco Zola

ZOLA IN LA DOLCE VITA

BY THE BEGINNING OF THE 1996-97 season things were starting to look bad for Gianfranco Zola at Parma. Manager Nevio Scala had left the club after seven successful years, and for Zola, who got on well with Scala, this was a big blow. Even worse for the tiny genius was that the new manager, Carlo Ancelotti, obviously didn't think Zola was part of Parma's long-term plan. The club's main strikers appeared to be Chiesa and Crespo, who both looked as though they were to be selected above Gianfranco Zola.

It was a worrying time for Zola, whose position looked under threat more than at any other period in his playing days for Parma. In the summer he had reached the age of 30 and had had a poor time in the European Championships just held in England. Perhaps Ancelotti thought Zola had seen his best days, but it was obvious to clubs looking for a talented player that if they had the money, Gianfranco Zola was available at the right price.

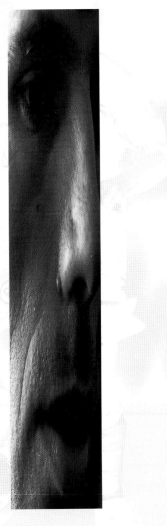

I was being made a scapegoat for all the team's problems and didn't want to stay to face up to the lies.
Gianfranco Zola, on his unhappy time at the end of his Parma career

I can say that in this year in Parma it was not the ideal condition for me. I can say in Parma I had a lot of problems in this year, so I decided to go and play here.
Gianfranco Zola

It should not have come to this point. The Parma team was not built to choose between me, Chiesa and Crespo; three for two places. In the programmes we should all three have played and without changing position. They saw that playing with three things weren't going well and they went back to two.

Gianfranco Zola

ONE CLUB ON the lookout for a player was Chelsea. The previous season, under now England manager Glenn Hoddle, the ambitious London club had approached Parma to see if they could buy Zola but were put off by the massive £8m asking rate.

He's a lovely player and I've always admired him. Technically he's right up there with the very best in Europe. I tried to sign him for Chelsea 18 months ago but they wanted £8m for him and I didn't have that sort of money.

Ex-Chelsea boss Glenn Hoddle

I had Di Matteo and Vialli and wasn't looking to buy another Italian. But when Zola became available it was an opportunity too good to miss. At Parma he was a victim of playing style. If they didn't want to use his ability I certainly wanted it.

Ruud Gullit

WHEN THE BLUES approached in November 1996, however, the timing was perfect. Ancelotti was willing to sell and the price had come down by almost £4m. On 8 November 1996, Chelsea, after press speculation, announced they had bought the Sardinian for £4.5m – a snip in today's transfer market prices. For Chelsea it was a major transfer coup and confirmed that under manager Ruud Gullit they were once again becoming one of England's glamour clubs. But for Zola it was a journey into the unknown.

I decided to join Chelsea because they believed in me and I wanted to be happy again. I thought it would be difficult for me to play in England because I am short and there are so many high balls. Chelsea are working hard to play the European way. The style of play was important to me.

Gianfranco Zola

Of all the cities I've been to London is the best. There's less poverty than in New York or Naples. I see my time here as completing my education as a footballer and as a person.

Gianfranco Zola

ALTHOUGH HE NEEDED a new challenge because of the situation at Parma, Zola was privately fearful that he might be too small for the more combative style of football played in England. In 1994, Zola's Parma played the European Cup Winners Cup Final against one of the most physical of English teams – George Graham's Arsenal. For Zola it wasn't a happy experience. The London club won 1-0 with a goal from Alan Smith and from the Sardinian there were only a few glimpses of genius as he was tightly marked. He was later to claim that every time a high ball was played to him, his marker – former England skipper Tony Adams – didn't even have to jump because Zola was so small!

He has the ability to win matches on his own and that is why I brought him to Stamford Bridge. I was never worried about his size – he may be small in stature but he is a giant in talent.
Chelsea boss Ruud Gullit

Zola's a better player than I thought he was. I was prepared to put my two full backs in forward positions and leave Pallister and Johnsen to look after Hughes and Zola. But Zola was smart enough to go wide and cause us a lot of problems. He's a clever little bugger.
Manchester United boss Alex Ferguson

ENGLISH FOOTBALL with its reliance on strength, commitment and height seemed the last place a pocket genius like Zola should be playing. And when he signed there were question marks over whether Zola could make the grade in England.

But at Chelsea under Ruud Gullit's expanding foreign legion of players, he was to find a team who tried to play European style football, and he was also shown that the English style of play was changing. The emphasis placed on attacking proved a godsend for Zola who found his career taking off again. The release from the football of Serie A, with its over-emphasis on tactics, had a transforming effect on Zola. Although he started the season off in the doldrums, by the end of 1996-97 Zola had completed one of the most successful years in his distinguished playing history.

The idea of going abroad is one I have always nurtured and every now and then I have talked about it with my wife. We are both ready to undertake this adventure.
Gianfranco Zola

I understand that Chelsea is a very beautiful area and I've just learnt there are some excellent Sardinian restaurants.
Gianfranco Zola

I enjoy living in London and it is all that I hoped it to be. You can't be bored in this city and my whole family love it here.
Gianfranco Zola

DESPITE CHELSEA pulling off a major transfer coup by signing Zola, his arrival in England should probably have been expected. The little Sardinian had been learning English, according to reports, for between one and four years.

If Zola never manages to conquer the English language he could still make himself understood in his own language on the football pitch. He has two fellow Italians alongside him at Chelsea – Gianluca Vialli and Roberto Di Matteo – manager Ruud Gullit speaks fluent Italian and Chelsea colleague Dan Petrescu used to play for Foggia and Genoa. Former Juventus star Attilio Lombardo plays for Crystal Palace and Stefan Eranio, once of Milan, now plays for Derby County. At least another five Premiership stars have played in Serie A and, of course, there is always Middlesbrough if Chelsea draw the Teesiders in the cup again. Indeed Zola says his major language problem is understanding Dennis Wise's English!

He may have kept me out of the side but I have nothing but praise for Gianfranco. He is a lovely player and a lovely man and we are a much better side with him at Chelsea.
Gianluca Vialli

If at the beginning of the season they had told me that I would have to change roles I would have discussed and probably we would have come to some kind of agreement. But these are things which should be worked out at the start.
Gianfranco Zola

I can't think of another foreign player who has made such an immediate impact on our game.
Dennis Wise, on Gianfranco Zola

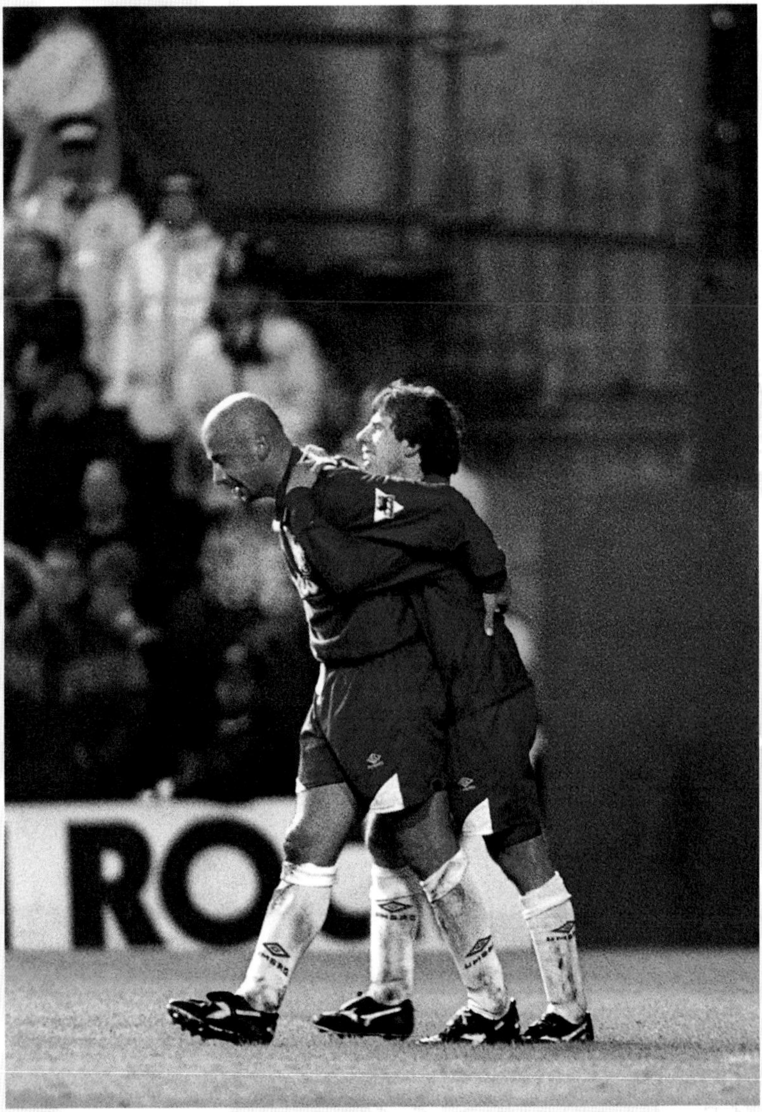
RO

ZOLA AT CHELSEA

FROM HIS VERY FIRST GAME for Chelsea, Zola stamped his Italian genius on the English game. He made his debut at Ewood Park, Blackburn, on 16 November 1996 and was voted Man of the Match despite the unfamiliarity of the surroundings. His home debut was made the following week when Chelsea took on championship contenders Newcastle United. The match was seen by millions all over the world as the game was broadcast all over Europe and beyond, even as far away as Tanzania. Those watching would have seen a typical piece of Zola skill from a free kick. In the 24th minute Chelsea were awarded a free kick about 25 yards out from the goal and just to the left of the Newcastle box. This was the first time Zola had a chance to show just what a different class player he was, and he didn't disappoint the expectant Chelsea fans. He whipped in an undefendable free kick with his right foot, which Italian colleague Gianluca Vialli easily touched into the net. The crowd went wild and although Chelsea only drew the game 1-1, the fans knew this was only the beginning of Zola's career in England. They knew they had a world-class match winner in their team – something they hadn't known for years – and defences up and down the land were given warning that they were going to be up against something special in the near future.

Adams didn't even have to jump to win the ball,
which is why I thought I'd be too small to play here,
that I have no chance against English defenders.
Gianfranco Zola, on an earlier encounter with Arsenal's Tony Adams

Chelsea in the first 15 minutes nearly had me falling
off the top of the stand. It looked like being a suicide job
because it was looking nasty for us, it could have been 5-0.
Sheffield Wednesday manager David Pleat,
on a Zola-inspired performance in December

ZOLA SCORED his first goal for Chelsea – naturally enough a 30-yard free kick – and created the second for Vialli in the 2-2 home draw against Everton on 7 December. In total he was to go on and score eight league goals, the same as his striking partner Mark Hughes and one behind the eventual top scorer Gianluca Vialli.

Gianluca Vialli told me how much I would enjoy myself here. There are many good things in Italian football, but also many bad things. The tension before matches and the need to win brings too much stress there.
Gianfranco Zola

ZOLA'S FORM WAS such that he presented a huge selection problem for manager Ruud Gullit. After only a few games it was obvious that he was indispensable, and with Gullit almost always refusing to play three up front, the final place was between Mark Hughes and Gianluca Vialli. Vialli lost out, his time on the substitutes bench due in part to his Italian colleague. Ironically, when he was in Italy, Gianfranco Zola had said that he was envious of Vialli because of the former Sampdoria and Juventus striker's charisma and popularity with the fans. Despite Vialli remaining a favourite with Chelsea fans, his popularity doesn't touch that of Zola's, who is revered as some sort of footballing god by the supporters at Stamford Bridge. Zola and Hughes went on to form one of the most feared partnerships in English football during the season: complementing each other with their vastly different styles of play. Zola now refers to Hughes as his minder on the pitch.

Even when I was in Italy I knew about Mark because he is such a famous player. When I am playing alongside I know I am going to have a good time because he helps me all the time.
Gianfranco Zola, on Mark Hughes

I just call Marco and Mark Hughes comes along and sorts everything out.
Gianfranco Zola, on his 'minder' Mark Hughes.

He's certainly added something to us and I know we're all delighted that he's here.
Mark Hughes

ON 21 DECEMBER, Zola came up against a defender with one of the most fearsome reputations in English football, Julian Dicks of West Ham United, and promptly dazzled him with a breathtaking piece of footballing wizardry, tying the Hammer's defender in knots before coolly slotting home for the game's second goal. Zola had already made the first for Mark Hughes. He scored both goals away against Aston Villa over Christmas. In December he was made the Carling Player of the Month. He also scored a marvellous volley against Sunderland, the first of six Chelsea put past the Wearsiders on 16 March. That was to be his final League goal of the season, but the tiny Italian had more than made his mark at Stamford Bridge. Through it all he played with a smile on his face. Zola was born to be a star. To round off the season he was voted the Football Writers' Association Player of the Year, the third consecutive time a foreign player had received the award.

*Zola was the difference.
We never got to grips with
him - and I feel we won't
be alone this season.*
**Brian Little, Aston Villa manager,
after Zola had scored both goals in
Chelsea's 2-0 victory**

*The Premiership now
has so many world class
players and the two
goals showed why it is
so popular in the rest
of Europe.*
**Ruud Gullit, after Zola's wonder goal
against Manchester United**

From the first day I've been touched by the atmosphere surrounding these matches. Here the supporters go to the stadium as if they were going to church. They come to commune with the players. The match is a festival, the chance to live a day in good humour.

Gianfranco Zola, on English fans

ZOLA AND THE FA CUP

THERE CAN BE LITTLE DOUBT that Gianfranco Zola was one of the stars, if not *the* star of English football during 1996-97. With his sublime dribbling skills, his long-range shooting, his clever football brain and his match-winning and crowd-pleasing abilities, it is not hard to see why Zola won so many plaudits last season from fans, players and managers.

His skills helped bring Chelsea their first piece of notable silverware for more than 26 years: the FA Cup. Not bad for a first season contribution – and it wasn't even a full season. If there was one place Zola seemed destined to finish the season it was at Wembley in May. And what competition could be better to bring the best out of Zola than the FA Cup. The world's most prestigious club event with over 125 years of history, and still one of the most glamorous football trophies to win. The cup still holds special significance in the English sporting calendar, much to Chelsea boss Ruud Gullit's bemusement, up there with the Grand National and Test series.

*I began this adventure with great
enthusiasm. I was ready to move mountains.
To be honest I thought I might have a bit of
trouble fitting into the team, to a football
that was new to me. In the end, everything
went ahead without any problems.*
Gianfranco Zola

*Winning the FA Cup was a big moment for me last
season and everyone is determined that we can go
on and challenge for the League title this season.*
Gianfranco Zola

THE BIG OCCASION, and Wembley in particular, seems to be one of Gianfranco Zola's favourite venues. He has now played there for Parma, Italy and Chelsea and has only left defeated on one occasion – the 1997 Charity Shield against Manchester United which Chelsea lost on penalties.

And of course the reason why Chelsea were appearing in this season's Charity Shield was because of their 2-0 victory in last May's Cup Final over Middlesbrough. A Cup victory in which Zola made a critical intervention and a Cup campaign in which his brilliance shone through in the depths of the dull English winter.

At times he was brilliant.
He's great to watch.
Former Liverpool and Scotland
defender Alan Hansen

The hallmark of a great player
is producing the goods when it
matters and he did just that.
Wimbledon manager Joe Kinnear,
after the FA Cup semi-final

HE SCORED IN every round bar two matches, but even when he wasn't scoring, his contribution was vital. His first ever Cup goal for Chelsea in their first tie, in the third round clash with West Bromwich Albion helped settle nerves and ease Chelsea into the fourth round for the tie of the competition and the game of the season. If Zola didn't know about the excitement of the English FA Cup before the game against Liverpool, he certainly did afterwards. On a bitter winter's day on 26 January, Zola was one of those who helped transform a certain defeat into probably Chelsea's greatest victory for many years, and reminded the older fans of the club's glory days back at the beginning of the 1970s. Stamford Bridge almost exploded when Zola equalised with a stunning 25-yard drive and helped Chelsea on the way to a famous 4-2 victory. Although he didn't score against Leicester City in the next round, he was on target again as Chelsea romped through their quarter-final clash with Portsmouth 4-1. In the semi-final against Wimbledon he created the first for Mark Hughes and scored another fantastic goal to put Chelsea in a commanding 2-0 lead. They eventually won 3-0.

Zola here is absolutely magnificent, that's a great flickback.
Alan Hansen, on Zola's crucial contribution to the 1997 FA Cup final

Zola flair lights up way to Wembley.
***Guardian* newspaper headline,**
after Gianfranco Zola's wonder-goal against
Wimbledon in the FA Cup semi-final

BEFORE THE FINAL, Zola was predicted to be one of the stars who could score the winner. But although the experts were wrong about that, he made one telling contribution, producing a fantastic back-heel to let Eddie Newton in to score the all-clinching second goal. Very few players could have so accurately or beautifully laid on the chance for Newton, but all fans were coming to expect the extraordinary at the very least from Zola. He also produced a marvellous dribbling run in a few seconds of magic, taking out most of the Middlesbrough defence.

And after Chelsea's victory, no-one looked happier than Gianfranco Zola as he paraded around Wembley with yet another winner's medal.

*This season has been
great for me, it's given
me great satisfaction.*
Gianfranco Zola, after Chelsea's FA Cup win

The match belonged to Zola.
**David Lacey, *Guardian* journalist, after the
Wimbledon Cup semi-final**

*I should have kept Zola at Parma
to play alongside Chiesa and
Crespo. We may have let in
more goals but we would have
scored a lot more as well. It was
definitely a mistake to let him
go but I am happy that he has
done so well for Chelsea.*
Carlo Ancelotti, Zola's former boss at Parma

ZOLA PLAYS FOR ITALY

NOT SURPRISINGLY FOR A PLAYER of his immense talent, Gianfranco Zola has represented his country – Italy – on many occasions. He has graced football fields all over the world wearing the colours of the Azzurri, playing in World Cup finals, USA 94, and Euro 96.

Although his time for the Italian side has been chequered, the confidence which has returned to his play since his transfer to Chelsea seems to have had a liberating effect on his national performances. Despite his successes with Chelsea, Zola is probably best known in this country for scoring the goal which may eventually prevent England from qualifying for the World Cup Finals in 1998 in France. Even though he may have put paid to England's hopes with the only goal of the game in February's World Cup qualifier at Wembley, he is still thought of warmly in this country. And his form with Chelsea has coincided with his rebirth at international level. At the beginning of 1997, Cesare Maldini replaced the controversial Arrigo Sacchi as Italian manager. For Zola, who had found himself in and out of Sacchi's sides like other flair players such as Roberto Baggio, Maldini's appointment has been yet another plus in a fantastic season for the Sardinian.

He is a very clever player, very astute. Apart from good technical ability, he reads the game so well. The best defenders can read the game when the opposition have the ball. Zola reads the game extremely well when his own side have it. He uses space very well.
England manager Glenn Hoddle

Zola was the pick of the bunch. He was very hard to mark, very hard to pick up. He caused us a lot of problems.
Northern Ireland international Steve Morrow, after playing in a friendly against Zola and Italy

GIANFRANCO ZOLA made his full Italian debut in November 1991 in Genoa when the Azzuri played Norway and drew 1-1. Despite his early successes in the Italian shirt, international life has been cruel to Zola on two memorable occasions in the past.

During the 1994 World Cup in the USA, Zola spent most of his time keeping the Italian bench warm as Sacchi put his faith in Roberto Baggio, despite several stuttering performances from the men in blue. When Zola did finally get on the pitch as a substitute, he lasted only 12 minutes after being dealt the cruellest of blows. Playing in the second round against Nigeria, Zola was the victim of a bizarre and over-zealous decision from a fussy Mexican referee who sent one of the world's cleanest players off for a late tackle on a Nigerian defender. The tackle was innocuous and it hardly seemed as if Zola had made contact with the Nigerian. Many wondered if it was even a free kick, let alone a sending off offence, but it was enough for Mr Arturo Brizio, the referee. It was the last action Zola was to see of the World Cup, despite the fact that Italy made the final where they lost to Brazil. To make matters worse, the sending off occurred on 5 July, 1994, Zola's 28th birthday!

I did not foul him. It meant I missed the rest of the World Cup. And I was more upset when the Secretary of FIFA, Sepp Blatter, said I deserved to be sent off.
Gianfranco Zola, on his controversial sending off during USA 94

I was gutted. I was supposed to have fouled one of their players. I mean, me, foul someone! It really upset me because I knew I was innocent and it was the end of my World Cup.
Gianfranco Zola

THE CURSE OF major championships returned to haunt
Gianfranco Zola during the Euro 96 tournament in England.
Although the tournament had started well, with Zola setting
up one of the Italians' goals in the victory over Russia, disaster
was to strike the Chelsea man soon afterwards. Wearing the
same number shirt, 21, as on that fateful day in the USA, Zola
had a chance to put Italy through to the next round when he
stepped up to take a penalty after a foul on Pierluigi
Casiraghi in the country's vital clash at Old Trafford against
Germany. Italy needed a victory to qualify, Germany just
needed a draw to be sure of qualification. His penalty was
the weakest one seen in this country since another Chelsea
player, Pat Nevin, just about reached the goalkeeper with a
penalty against Manchester City in 1984. German goalkeeper
Andreas Kopke saved easily and that was Italy's last chance.
The game finished 0-0 and Italy were eliminated to much
public anger, with plenty vented at Zola for his penalty miss.

Many things have changed since Sacchi left. We work with more serenity, we feel more loved with Maldini. We can recover our harmony and mend our relationship with the fans.
Gianfranco Zola, on the new international manager Cesare Maldini

In football there are no secrets.
Gianfranco Zola

BUT ALL CAME good for Zola on 12 February 1996, at Wembley, when Zola's goal from 12 yards, following exquisite control, was enough to give Italy three points in a vital Group Two game. It was England's first ever defeat at Wembley in a world cup qualifier. It was the first time Zola had started an international in the season and for good measure he scored another goal against Moldova in Italy's next match. In total, Gianfranco Zola has played 33 times for Italy, scoring 10 goals.

When I was young I always dreamed of scoring at Wembley. It is very important for me what has happened tonight.
Gianfranco Zola, after his goal gave Italy a 1-0 victory at Wembley over England

I put myself in the right position to score because of this.
Gianfranco Zola

Zola is just class. He is frightening sometimes. England will definitely have to man-mark. Even then he can still hurt you.
Chelsea captain Dennis Wise

ZOLA'S GOAL-DEN BOOTS

HOWEVER LONG HE STAYS IN English football, Gianfranco Zola's mark on the game over here has already been vast, despite the fact that he is yet to complete a full season for Chelsea. His popularity with English football fans, and not just Chelsea fans, seems secure.

His skills, his way of playing melt the hearts of the crowd.
Chelsea manager Ruud Gullit

The English are more difficult to conquer than the Italians. Day after day you have to show your worth.
Gianfranco Zola

EVEN THOUGH there have been some people moaning within England about the standard of some of the foreign players coming to play in the Premiership – 'Carlos Kickaballs' – as one chairman called them, no-one would put Zola in that category.

In fact after just one season, Zola already belongs to a club of foreign stars who have made an ever-lasting impact on English football, including Eric Cantona, Jürgen Klinsmann, Zola's Chelsea manager Ruud Gullit, and, further back, players like Osvaldo Ardiles and Arnold Muhren.

Without doubt Vialli, for the charisma that he gives out and the ability to galvanise others with his example.
Gianfranco Zola, asked in Italy in December 1995 about which current player he admires and is envious of

I am more confident now than I have ever been. Perhaps it is because I am playing better than I have done for a long while but it is also down to the fact that I feel at home at Chelsea.
Gianfranco Zola

There may be question marks over some of the others [foreign imports] but little 'Franco' is the real deal.
Sunday Times journalist Joe Lovejoy

THE REASON ZOLA is held in such high regard is simply because he is so exciting. He can do things with a football which set him apart from others and despite his small stature make him a giant on the football pitch. Because of his range and the breathtaking quality of his goals he has instantly become a favourite. When he scores it rarely seems to be ordinary, and is more likely to be from 25 yards rather than five yards. He scores the kind of goals fans can only dream of scoring and usually saves them for the big occasion.

Hugely skilled and utterly charming.
Total Sport magazine, September 1997

I can be better. I can be more effective for the team.
Gianfranco Zola

HIS CONTRIBUTION to Chelsea's FA Cup success was massive, already he is a Chelsea legend and he really is the kind of footballer who draws in the crowds when he gets the ball. Many of the best moments from the 1996-97 season involved Gianfranco Zola. At times he was simply irresistible. Above everything else, fans love skilful footballers, and long after Zola has retired, many in both Italy and England will have memories of his massive contribution to the art of football.

*Ruud has given me the opportunity to complete
my football life. All players should go to other
countries if they can to complete their education.
The English should try Italy, Germany or Spain.
Don't be afraid to try something new.*
Gianfranco Zola

*I think he's one of the most exciting players I've
seen. He's got two great feet. He plays with a
smile on his face. He's capable of producing
something out of nothing.*
Graham Rix, Chelsea's coach

SOME OF THOSE goals will be replayed for
years. Against Liverpool in the game of the
season, Chelsea's 4-2 victory in the FA Cup 4th
round after being 2-0 down, Zola struck a
magnificent 25-yard in to the top left-hand
corner to level the scores, with Liverpool
goalkeeper David James helpless. In the League
against champions Manchester United, Zola beat
two international defenders Denis Irwin and Gary
Pallister with an effortless dribble before coolly
beating one of the world's best goalkeepers
Peter Schmeichel at his near post.

Zola Power!
Popular flag flown by Chelsea fans throughout the 1996-97 season

It is so easy to play upfront alongside Mark Hughes. He is a world class player and creates openings for me by taking many defenders away, giving me the space to play. He is also my minder on the pitch and can sort out any trouble.

Gianfranco Zola

ON A COLD MARCH evening at Stamford Bridge he repeated his shot against Liverpool to score the only goal in a 1-0 victory over Southampton. But perhaps one of the best moments of the season was Zola's classy goal in the FA Cup semi-final which saw off Wimbledon. Receiving a pass on the edge of the box, Zola, running to his left, back-flicked the ball with his heel and changed the direction he was running all in one movement. Having lost his marker Dean Blackwell with speed of feet and mind, he then shot accurately from about 20 yards into the bottom right-hand corner. It put Chelsea well on the way to Wembley and confirmed the little Sardinian's genius. It was one of the champagne moments of the season – and there's no doubt there's more on the way.

At 30 he must feel reborn. The move to Stamford Bridge has revived his zest for the game and he has charmed everyone lucky enough to get the chance to watch him in a Chelsea shirt.

Guardian journalist, on Zola

I'd like to thank everybody for their support. The whole season has been fantastic.

Gianfranco Zola on his first season for Chelsea

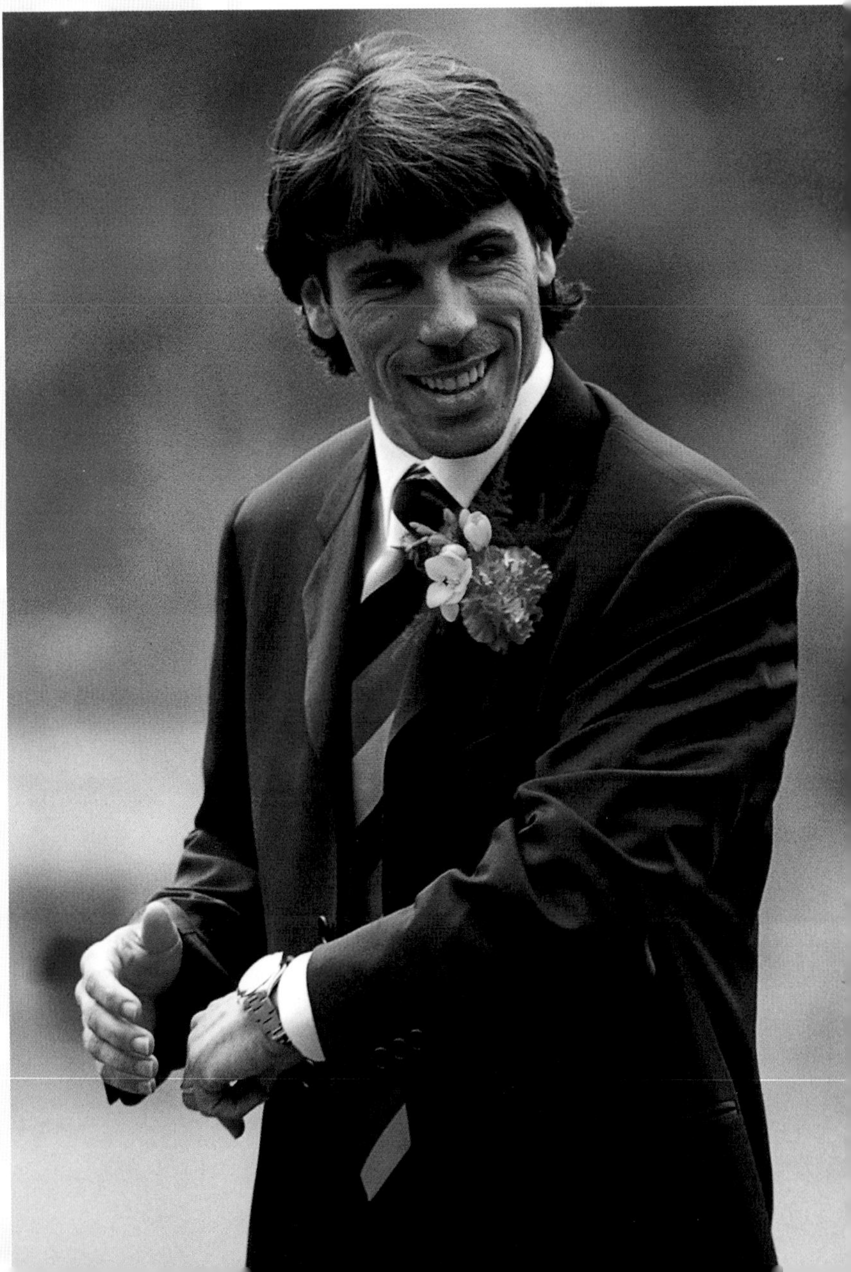

WHAT NEXT FOR THE INCREDIBLE ITALIAN?

GIANFRANCO ZOLA'S PLACE IN ENGLISH football history is assured, but what is not so certain is where he will be playing football after the World Cup in France in 1998. His contract at Chelsea, worth a reputed £25,000 a week, finishes at the end of the 1997-98 season. The Sardinian has made noises about returning to the island of his birth to finish his career, saying Italy is the country where he should retire and there is no doubt he still has a burning desire to play for Cagliari. But he has also said he may be prepared to play for longer than two years at Chelsea.

*In England teams are always looking to score,
to press forward. In Italy they would not
believe some of the things that happen here.
Vialli told me Chelsea were losing 5-0 and
Frank Leboeuf scores, then all the supporters
are willing him to score again in the last
minutes!*
Gianfranco Zola

*In London you can walk about
calmly in the streets; no-one
bothers you or follows you for hours.*
Gianfranco Zola

HIS AMBITION at the London club is to win
the Premiership title: a realistic possibility given
the additions to the squad made over the
summer by manager Ruud Gullit. If the title takes
a little longer, it might be that Zola can be
persuaded to stay at Stamford Bridge.

Chelsea are also in Europe this season, in
the European Cup Winners' Cup and have their
FA Cup to defend, so whatever happens the
Sardinian will be busy.

*It is a luxury, every coach
should have that problem.*
Ruud Gullit, on his selection problems caused by Gianfranco Zola

Delicate moves and technical exploits are much appreciated here. And yet it's customary to say that British football is wholly athletic and committed to extremes.
Gianfranco Zola

BUT HIS MOST important match in the 1997-98 season will be the World Cup qualifier in Rome against the country he has taken to so easily, England, on 11 November. Whoever wins will automatically qualify for the finals in France in the summer, but for the losers there could be heartbreak. For Zola the chance to play in another World Cup would be a dream, especially considering the heartbreak of the last tournament in the USA. Now aged 31, France probably represents the last chance for Zola to show the world his phenomenal skills.

Scoreflash coming in......it's Emile Zola again for Chelsea.
Radio 5 gets it wrong

I like the idea of playing abroad to further my experience and think everyone should try it. We have a united Europe, so people should not be afraid to try something new.
Gianfranco Zola

He's built himself up to be strong enough to cope with this fast football. After training he always does stretches and other things and that makes him the player he is now. He did it himself.
Ruud Gullit

GIANFRANCO ZOLA

BUT WHATEVER happens to him during the course of the season, there is little doubt that he will continue to endear himself to English football fans. His subtle touches of skill, his blistering free-kicks and shots and his huge smile will long guarantee him a place in the hearts of English football fans, who may eventually forgive him for scoring that goal at Wembley. Far from fearing for the little Italian, fans now know that he can do more than just hold his own in the hurly burly world of English League football surpassing the achievements of almost all the foreign imports who have played in England. When eventually he does leave England he will leave behind a host of memories of Zola in full flight which he will no doubt add to throughout this season. The English game would be poorer without him.

After the game the two teams always meet in the bar and all the bad things are forgotten. I don't drink but I like the idea of people meeting together. In Italy people would look at me strange if I congratulated an opponent.
Gianfranco Zola

Franco is one of those players who brings strikers like me good fortune.
Gianluca Vialli, who Zola replaced in the Chelsea team

My wife Franca is very happy. We are both here to stay. We will live in London for the next four years.
Gianfranco Zola

84

FACT FILE

- *Full Name*:
  Gianfranco Zola
- *Height*:
  5' 5"
- *Weight*:
  10st 3lb
- *Born*:
  5 July 1966 in Oliena, Sardinia
- *Career*:
  Nuorese from 5 July 1982, a C2 team (Italian equivalent of Division Three). In his first season, he appears in 31 games, scoring 10 goals.

  Torres from 1986 onwards. One season after Zola's arrival, the club makes it to C1. Zola plays 88 games for Torres, shooting 21 goals.

  Napoli pay £200,000 in 1989 for Gianfranco. In 106 games he scores 32 goals.

  Parma, one of Northern Italy's premier teams, pay £1.4 million in 1993. Zola plays a total of 140 games, scoring 62 goals. Becomes disenchanted when forced to play a more defensive role after the arrival of Enrico Chiesa and Hernan Crespo.

  Chelsea from 8 November 1996. Zola's worth is now £4.5 million. By the end of 1996-97, Zola has played 23 games for his new team, claiming 8 goals.

ZOLA'S GOLDEN MOMENTS

- Plays as a substitute for Diego Maradona at Napoli. When Maradona leaves in 1991, Gianfranco takes over from him.
- At Parma, often quoted as one of the best mezzapunta (attacking mid-fielders) in the League.
- 1994-5 Parma team record for highest number of goals scored in a season (19).
- Gianfranco was the third highest goal scorer in Serie A after Bastituta and Signori.
- 1996-97 Zola makes an immediate impact on the Premiership culminating in the FA Cup win against Middlesbrough.

ZOLA & ITALY

- *13 November 1992*
  Zola makes his Italian debut against Norway in Genoa (1-1)
- *USA 94*
  Mistakenly sent off against Nigeria.
- *12 February 1996*
  Gianfranco Zola scores a spectacular goal – from 12 yards. He is battling against England, and his superb play gives Italy three points in a vital Group Two game. It is Zola's goal which helps towards England's first ever defeat in a World Cup qualifier at Wembley.
- In October 1996, Italy beat Moldova 3-1 and Georgia 1-0.
- Gianfranco Zola has earned 33 full caps for his country, notching up 10 international goals.

TRANSFERS

- **1984**
  At the young age of 18, Gianfranco Zola joins Nuorese, a small club in his native country of Sardinia.
- **1986**
  Aged 20, Zola makes the move to Italy and the Torres team.
- **1989**
  Napoli pay £200,000 for a Zola transfer. Gianfranco realises a life's ambition with the chance to play alongside his childhood hero and inspiration – football ace, Diego Maradona.
- **1993**
  Zola's transfer fee multiplies sevenfold and Gianfranco heads north to join Parma – for £1.4 million.
- **1995**
  Glenn Hoddle, manager of Chelsea, approaches Parma to make a bid for Zola. The Italians ask for £8 million – the price is too high.
- **8 November 1996**
  A year of negotiations later, Zola, aged 30, transfers to Chelsea for £4.5 million.

ZOLA'S HONOURS

- December 1996 - after Gianfranco's first full month with Chelsea he is named Player of the Month. Gianfranco receives a trophy, a magnum of champagne and a cheque for £250.
- 1997 Zola is voted Football Writers' Association Player of the Year. Gianfranco follows Jürgen Klinsmann (1995) and Eric Cantona (1996).

CHELSEA

- Ground: Stamford Bridge, London, SW6 1HS.
- Ground capacity: 31,544.
- Pitch measurements: 113 yd x 74 yd.
- Year formed: 1905.
- Founders: Mr H. A. Mears & Mr Frederick Parker.
- Nicknames: 'The Blues'.
- Current sponsors: Autoglass
- Greatest rivals: Formerly Tottenham, but Chelsea have a 17-year unbroken run of victories against them; now Manchester United.
- Celebrity fans: Roddy Doyle, Sir Richard Attenborough, David Mellor, David Baddiel, Sebastian Coe, John Major & Tony Banks
- Fans favourite: Gianfranco Zola
- It's true: In the 1996-97 season Chelsea used five different goalies, all of different nationalities.
- Weirdest merchandise: Italjet scooters in Chelsea Blue.
- Greatest score: 13-0 v Jeunnesse Hautcharage (Cup Winners' Cup 1971).
- Record defeat: 1-8 v Wolverhampton Wanderers (Division 1 1923).
- Leading goalscorers in one season (then/now): Jimmy Greaves (1960-61) 43/Mark Hughes 14.
- Record Transfer paid: £4.9 million for Roberto Di Matteo (from Lazio, August 1996).
- Record Transfer received: £2.5 million for John Spencer (QPR, November 1996) and £2.5 million for Craig Burley (Celtic, July 1997).

Record attendance at a Chelsea match was on 12 October 1935, when 82,905 fans watched Chelsea v Arsenal (Division One).

- Best Website: http://chelseaafc.co.uk (official) & http://home.sol.no/roaaune
- Stamford Bridge was built before there was a team to play in it. Originally, the ground was offered to Fulham but they decided to use Craven Cottage instead.
- Even in the twenties and the thirties Chelsea were known for the club's high spending on players, this was reflected by the huge attendance at games.
- Big success came in the 1970s with the arrival of Dave Sexton. Victory in the FA Cup in 1970 and the European Cup Winners' Cup in 1971 were the last honours until 1997.
- Players such as Osgood, Bonetti, Hudson, Hutchinson and Cooke are still legends.
- The massive East Stand was built in the late seventies, leading to serious financial troubles for the club. Many key players were sold to pay off debts. As a result, Chelsea ended up being relegated.
- Chelsea regained First Division status in 1985 after 5 years in the Second Division.
- Chelsea were relegated for one season in 1989. They climbed back to the top flight with a record 99 points and 96 goals.
- 1993 Glenn Hoddle arrived and had an immediate impact on Chelsea.
- 1994 FA Cup final appearance.
- In 1995, Chelsea made it to the European Cup Winners' Cup semi-final.

- On 17 June 1996, Chelsea's popular player-manager Ruud Gullit signed a new contract to take him to 1998, with a further two-year option to be discussed later.
- On 24 June 1996, Ruud Gullit agreed a [then] record club fee of £2.5 million to buy French defender Frank Leboeuf from Racing Club Strasbourg.

- On 27 August 1996, Chelsea beat Wimbledon 2-0 to a barrage of applause from a rapturous crowd of fans.
- 18 September 1996, Chelsea played Blackpool. After a potentially disastrous goal from Blackpool in the first minute of the game, Chelsea came back with a vengeance, not allowing any more goals to slip past the keeper and winning with a score of 4-1.
- On 23 October 1996, tragic news was broken: popular Chelsea director, and multi-millionaire, Matthew Harding, was killed in a helicopter crash, along with the pilot and three other passengers. The club, players and fans were devastated. In memory of the great man, a stand at Stamford Bridge is now named the Matthew Harding Stand. After his death,Chelsea and Spurs fans paid tribute before their match – appropriately Chelsea won 3-1.

THE CURRENT CHELSEA SQUAD

- Goal-keepers: Ed De Goey (Dutch Number One with 29 caps) previous club Sparta Rotterdam. Signed by Gullit for £2.25 million. Kevin Hitchcock (English) previous clubs Barking, Nottingham Forest, Mansfield Town & Northampton Town (on loan). Frode Grodas (Norwegian international with 30 caps) previous club Lillestrom. Dimitri Kharine (Russian international with 34 caps) previous club CSKA Moscow.
- Defenders: Dan Petrescu (Romanian international wing back with 54 caps) previous clubs Genoa and Sheffield Wednesday. Celestine Babayaro (Nigerian international with 12 caps) previous club Anderlecht. Signed for £2.25 million. Frank Leboeuf (French international) previous clubs Strasbourg, Hyeres, Meaux & Laval. Steve Clarke (Scottish with 6 caps) previous clubs Beith Juniors & St Mirren. Bernard Lambourde (Guadalope/French) previous clubs Bourdeaux & AS Cannes. Michael Duberry (English Under-21 squad) signed as a Trainee but had a spell on loan to Bournemouth. Graham

Le Saux (Channel Islander/England with 20 caps) previous clubs Jersey, Chelsea & Blackburn Rovers. David Lee (English with 10 Under-21 caps) previous clubs Reading (loan), Plymouth (loan) & Portsmouth (loan). Danny Granville (English) previous club Cambridge United. Frank Sinclair (English) previous club West Bromwich Albion (loan). Neil Clement (English Schools, Youth and Under-18 international) signed from Trainee.

- Mid-fielders: Ruud Gullit (Surinam/Dutch with 64 caps) previous clubs Haarlem, PSV Endhoven, AC Milan & Sampdoria. Only 12 appearances in 1995-96 season has probably hung up his boots to concentrate on managing the team. Gustavo Poyet (Uruguayan with 23 caps) previous club Real Zaragoza. Dennis Wise (English with 12 caps) previous club Wimbledon. Roberto Di Matteo (Swiss, but Italian international) previous clubs Lazio, Schaffausen, Zurich & Aarau. Jody Morris (English international Under-17 captain) signed from Trainee. Eddie Newton (English Under-21) previous club Cardiff City (loan).
- Utility players: Andy Myers (English with 3 Under-21 caps) signed from a Trainee.
- Forwards - Gianfranco Zola (Italian international with 33 caps) previous clubs Nuorese, Torres, Napoli & Parma. Gianluca Vialli (Italian with 59 caps) previous clubs Cremonese, Sampdoria & Juventus. Mark Hughes (Welsh with 65 caps) previous clubs Manchester United, Barcelona & Bayern Munich (on loan). Signed for 1.5 million. Tore Andre Flo (Norwegian international with 15 caps) previous club SK Brann Bergen. Signed for £300,000. Mark Nicholls (English) signed from Trainee.

- Who's bad: Frank Leboeuf (seven yellow and one red cards during 1996-97 season).
- One to watch: Steve Clarke.

ACKNOWLEDGEMENTS

Introduction by Robert Jeffery.
Robert Jeffery worked on local newspapers before helping to launch *Sky Sports Magazine*. He is currently a reporter on *FourFourTwo*, Britain's best-selling football magazine. He supports Wimbledon and Slough Town.

Main text by David Harding.
David Harding is a lifelong Chelsea supporter and has worked as a journalist for newspapers, television and magazines (including *Kick It City* and *The Chelsea Independent*). His proudest footballing moment came when he was selected for Southampton Schoolboys – he was dropped after just one game. His ambition is to see Everton relegated.

Fact file compiled by Jon Sutherland.

The Foundry would like to thank Helen Burke, Helen Courtney, Helen Johnson, Lucinda Hawksley, Lee Matthews, Morse Modaberi and Sonya Newland for all their work on this project.

Picture Credits
All pictures © copyright Empics Sports Photo Agency